"THE SKIES PR

DELIGHTING IN GOD'S LAW

BARRY L. ROSS

Paperback edition ISBN:

E-book edition ISBN:

Paperback and eBook copies available on: Amazon.com

Dedication

I dedicate this book to
my lovely wife Dorcas, who loves God's written Word,
delightfully searches out its truths, and lives them
in her daily walk.

About the Author

Barry L. Ross is an ordained minister in The Wesleyan Church. He holds degrees from Houghton College (NY), Asbury Theological Seminary (KY), The University of Michigan (MI), and Drew University (NJ). He specialized in Old Testament and Biblical Hebrew and related ancient near eastern languages. He taught 23 years in undergraduate and graduate ministry education in America and 20 years in Bible Colleges and seminaries in Japan and other Asia and Pacific countries. He is now retired, living in Brooksville, FL, with his wife Dorcas.

Other Books by the Author

Barry L. Ross. 2023. *Daniel.* Reading and Interpreting the Bible Series. Kansas City: The Foundry Publishing.

Barry L. Ross. 2016. *Isaiah 1–39, A Commentary in the Wesleyan Tradition.* New Beacon Bible Commentary Series. Kansas City: Beacon Hill Press.

David L. Thompson, Barry L. Ross, Alex Varughese. 2020. *Psalms 73–150, A Commentary in the Wesleyan Tradition.* New Beacon Bible Commentary Series. Kansas City: Beacon Hill Press.

Alex Varughese, Barry L. Ross, Robert D. Branson. 2021. *Numbers, A Commentary in the Wesleyan Tradition.* New Beacon Bible Commentary Series. Kansas City: Beacon Hill Press.

Contents

Bibliography

Ahmad, Mariam. March 30, 2023. "Ten Most Expensive Precious Metals," *Mining Digital Magazine.* https://miningdigital.com. Accessed August 28, 2023.

Goldingay, John. 2008. *Psalms Vol. 3: Psalms 90–150.* Baker Commentary on the Old Testament Wisdom and Psalms. Edited by Tremper Longman III. Grand Rapids: Baker Academic.

Hartley, John E. 1988. *The Book of Job.* New International Commentary on the Old Testament. General Editor, R. K. Harrison. Grand Rapids: Eerdmans.

Thompson, David L. 2015. *Psalms 1-72, A Commentary in the Wesleyan Tradition.* New Beacon Bible Commentary. Kansas City: Beacon Hill Press.

Thompson, David L., Barry L. Ross and Alex Varughese. 2020 *Psalms 73-150, A Commentary in the Wesleyan Tradition.* New Beacon Bible Commentary. Kansas City: Beacon Hill Press.

Voynick, Steve. April 3, 2023. "Minerals & Metals of the Bible," *Rock&Gem.* https://www.rockngem.com. Accessed August 28, 2023.

Preface

In 2005, Fountain Press of Pune, India, published my book of studies on selected biblical Psalms entitled *Musing with David.* That selection of studies ranged more widely throughout the book of Psalms than does this present book. The 2005 publication is now out of print and no longer available, and the publisher has committed the original copyright to me.

In this present publication, *Delighting in God's Law,* I have selected and significantly revised my original studies on Psalms 1, 19 and 119. These three psalms speak of the delight and benefits of following God's law. As you read, I trust you may gain spiritual insight and find encouragement for your own journey on life's pathway.

"Delight" in Psalms 1, 19 and 119 (NIV)

"Blessed is the one . . . whose delight is in the law of the LORD" (1:1-2).

"I delight in your decrees; I will not neglect your word" (119:16).

"Your statutes are my delight; they are my counselors" (119:24).

"Direct me in the path of your commands, for there I find delight" (119:35).

"I delight in your commands because I love them" (119:47).

"Their hearts are callous and unfeeling, but I delight in your law" (119:70).

"Let your compassion come to me that I may live, for your law is my delight" (119:77).

"If your law had not been my delight, I would have perished in my affliction" (119:92).

"Trouble and distress have come upon me, but your commands give me delight" (119:143).

"I long for your salvation, LORD, and your law gives me delight" (119:174).

Introduction

In this small book I present 30 studies on *Psalms 1, 19* and *119*. These three psalms highlight how God's law guides us as followers of God throughout our life's journey.

Psalm 1 is an anonymous author's six-verse observation of two types of persons. One type scoffs (v. 1) at God's law, while living a lifestyle that boasts, "God law doesn't apply to me!" The other type embraces God's law into all aspects of daily life, while delighting (v. 2) in living a lifestyle that says, "God's law *is* for me!" At the close of one's earthly life, the lifestyle each has lived does matter, affirms the author, for God *knows* (or, watches) both, and God determines the final judgment concerning each one's continuing existence on into eternity (v. 6).

Psalm 19 is King David's fourteen-verse testimony that the very heavens—God's visible law in the skies!—declare God's glory (v. 1). David includes in his testimony that God's written law gives wisdom to the person who fears the Lord, and that God's law makes one's heart rejoice (vv. 7-9). God's law, he says, is to be desired more than riches ("gold," v. 10). Moreover, to the one who keeps God's law, there is great reward (v. 11).

Psalm 119 is an anonymous author's 176-verse meditation upon God's written law (v. 1). It is from this law that you and I can discover the standard by which we can know and walk in God's will. We can pray with our psalmist that God will open our spiritual eyes so that we may see the wonderful things found in his law (v. 18). We learn that God will direct us in his will which he reveals to each of us individually, if we pray, as our psalmist prays, for God's direction into the way of his commands, for indeed we will find delight in those commands (v. 35).

1

Delighting in the Law of the Lord

> *1 Blessed is the one who does not walk in step with the wicked or stand in the way that sinners take or sit in the company of mockers, 2 but whose delight is in the law of the LORD, and who meditates on his law day and night.*
>
> **Psalm 1:1-2**

In Psalm 1, our psalmist presents two groups of persons, and the path and attitude each has chosen in life regarding God's law. One group features the "blessed" persons (v. 1), or the "righteous" (v. 6). The other group features the "wicked," "sinners" or "mockers" (vv. 1, 4, 5, 6).

In verse 1, our psalmist tells us what persons of the first group, the "blessed" persons do *not* do.

First, they do not "walk in step with the wicked." "Wicked" is a general term for unbelievers. It is unthinkable for a blessed person to seek advice from an unbeliever concerning the conduct of one's life.

Second, blessed persons do not "stand in the way that sinners take." The Hebrew for "sinners" implies those who, either ignorantly or deliberately, are *failing* to obey God.

Third, blessed persons do not "sit in the company of mockers." Other English versions fittingly translate the Hebrew for "mockers" as "scoffers." "Scoffers" defines the specific *kind* of sin of which mockers are guilty: *they scoff at God's law*. The scoffer admits that God exists, but insists, "God and his law have nothing to do with me! I live my life according to my own plan." The scoffer is the same as the "fool" of Psalm 14, of whom psalmist David says, "The fool says in his heart, 'There is no God.' They are corrupt, their deeds are vile. . . . Do all these evildoers know nothing? They devour my people as though eating bread; they never call on the LORD" (vv. 1, 4). Moreover, they are like the "wicked" of Psalm 73, of whom psalmist Asaph says, "They scoff, and speak with malice; with arrogance they threaten oppression. . . . They say, 'How would God know? Does the Most High know anything?'" (vv. 3, 8, 11).

So, insists our psalmist of Psalm 1, "blessed" persons, those who enjoy God's favor, do *not* find life's direction in the counsel of such persons!

In verse 2, our psalmist tells us what blessed persons *do*.

First, that which the scoffer finds no use for—"the law of the LORD"—a blessed person finds to be an absolute "delight." This implies much more than merely a happy feeling. The Hebrew verb means to "desire for," "wish for," or "take joy in" something. The adjective describes something that is "precious," something held dear to one's heart.

Second, a blessed person's response of delight to God's law is all-consuming: life is governed by "his law day and night"—virtually all the time! Our psalmist expresses this all-consuming activity with the term "meditates." This term implies more than merely *thinking* about God's law. The Hebrew term carries the meanings to "mutter," "speak" and "proclaim." Thus, our psalmist is saying that God's teachings about how life is to be lived so consumes blessed persons that they cannot stop speaking them or talking about them day and night. The heart of our psalmist of Psalm 1 would surely resonate with our psalmist of Psalm 119, who testifies, "At midnight I rise to give you thanks for your righteous laws. . . . I delight in your law (119:62, 70).

Pray: Dear Lord, my heavenly Father, as I walk today in obedience to your law, I ask that, with the help of your indwelling Holy Spirit, I may find joy and *delight* in doing your will. I pray this in the Name of Jesus. *Amen.*

2

Transplanted by Canals

> *3 That person is like a tree planted by streams of water, which yields its fruit in season and whose leaf does not wither—whatever they do prospers. 4 Not so the wicked! They are like chaff that the wind blows away.*
>
> **Psalm 1:3-4**

In Psalm 1:3-4, our psalmist *contrasts* the blessed and wicked persons introduced in Psalm 1:1.

In verse 3, our psalmist tells us what the blessed person is "like." Such a person "is like a tree planted by streams of water." Our psalmist has set aside the usual Hebrew word to "plant" and has deliberately chosen "*trans*plant." Moreover, he has passed over the Hebrew word for a natural "stream" that flows wherever it will and has chosen the word for a man-made irrigation "canal." Such a canal receives its flow of water from a reservoir, which has received *its* reserve of water from either a river or the rains during the rainy season. So, even during the dry season when there are no rains, the farmer may release water into his irrigation system, giving life supporting nourishment to the plants and trees that he has planted along its canals.

The "tree" in the metaphor of verse 3 perhaps had sprung up by chance from a seed carried by the wind to a place with water only during the rainy season. But, when the rainy season had passed, its source of life-sustaining water was drying up. The farmer, upon finding this special tree and wishing to preserve it and grow it to maturity, has carefully dug it up and *trans*planted it beside one of his irrigation canals. There, it finds a continuous source of life-sustaining water.

Our psalmist is teaching us that, just as this transplanted "tree" continuously draws its life-sustaining nurture from the irrigation canal, just so the "blessed" person draws spiritually life-sustaining nurture from God's "law day and night" (v. 2). The water that nourishes the roots of the blessed person consists of the teachings gleaned from "the law of the LORD."

Moreover, our psalmist does not measure blessed persons' prosperity by possessions acquired, nor by their rise through political ranks to top positions. Rather, the prosperity of blessed persons is *spiritual.* Whatever the weather or climate, blessed persons have a look of *spiritual* health—they are those who produce "fruit in season," and "whose leaf" is not withered.

In verse 4, our psalmist exclaims, "Not so the wicked!" "Not so" what? one might ask. "The wicked," our psalmist is declaring, are not like blessed persons.

Our psalmist then introduces a new element—"the wind." Though unstated, the wind points back at what our psalmist has said earlier about the blessed person, whom the tree symbolizes. When the wind blows, the transplanted tree/blessed person may bend one way or the other, but with deep roots, it neither breaks nor uproots. When the wind ceases, it still stands!

"Not so the wicked! They are like chaff." Chaff is that useless light-weight husk that remains mixed with the threshed grain piled on the threshing floor, and must be separated from the grain. "The wind" now points to "the wicked," whom the chaff symbolizes. On a windy day, the farmer throws the grain into the air, again and again, until the wind has blown away all that chaff! Such, says our psalmist, is the outcome God has planned for the wicked, as we will see in v. 6.

Pray: Dear Lord, my heavenly Father. Enable me to become so deeply rooted in knowledge and practice of your law, that I may be able to stand firm when the winds of evil blow against me. I ask this in the Name of Jesus. *Amen.*

3

God Knows!

> *5 Therefore the wicked will not stand in the judgment, nor sinners in the assembly of the righteous. 6 For the LORD watches over the way of the righteous, but the way of the wicked leads to destruction.*
>
> **Psalm 1:5-6**

Here, our psalmist reveals life's final outcome for both blessed persons and the wicked. Earlier in this psalm, blessed persons are those who have chosen *not* to allow their life's path to be guided by the thinking and decisions of the community of the wicked, those who mock or scoff at God's law (v. 1). Scoffers are people who have rejected God's law as having anything to do with their chosen way of life.

In verse 5, these same "wicked," declares our psalmist, will not be found "in the judgment, nor in the assembly of the righteous." The "righteous" are the blessed persons of verse 1, those who have chosen to allow "the law of the LORD " to govern their lifestyles.

While we cannot know for sure the mind of our psalmist, it is possible that by "the judgment" and "the assembly of the righteous," he "refers to end-times judgment and life" (Thompson 2015, 72) The Greek translation of the Old

Testament (the Septuagint) reads, "sinners will not rise again," while the Aramaic translation (the Targum) reads, "The wicked will not be pure in the great day"(Thompson 2015, 72).

In verse 6, our psalmist reveals the ignorance of "the wicked," who, in another psalm scoffingly said, " 'How would God know? Does the Most High know anything?' " (Ps. 73:3, 8, 11).

"Oh, yes, indeed, he does!" our psalmist of Psalm 1 would reply. While the NIV translates, "The LORD *watches over* the way of the righteous," the Hebrew literally says, "The LORD *knows*" (v. 6, my emphasis). David Thompson observes that God's knowing implies that God is both cognitively aware of the *actions* of the righteous, and that it is God's "participation in the life of the righteous that accounts for life as they experience it" (Thompson 2015, 72).

On a comparative note, in Psalm 139:1-3, psalmist David uses four different verbs for God's knowing, each deeper than the preceding one. First, God is aware of David's actions inside his house: "you *know* when I sit and when I rise." Second, God is aware of what goes on inside David himself: "you *perceive* my thoughts." Third, God is aware of what goes on outside David's house: "You *discern* my going out and my lying down." Fourth, there is nothing about David's life that escapes God's notice: "you are *familiar* with all my ways" (my emphasis). Thus, David recognizes God's full participation in his life.

Returning to Psalm 1, our psalmist says, "the LORD watches over the way of the righteous" (v. 6). As I noted above, the Hebrew is literally "the LORD *knows*" (my emphasis). Though our psalmist applies God's knowing only to the lifestyle of the righteous, he implies that God knows the lifestyles of *both* the righteous and the wicked.

Earlier, I noted the wicked of Psalm 73, who, in the midst of their wickedness, sneeringly asked, "Does the Most High know anything?" (v. 11). Psalmist Asaph's response to their sneer was, "Surely you [God] place them on slippery ground; you cast them down to ruin. How suddenly they are destroyed, completely swept away by terrors! . . . Those who are far from you will perish; you destroy all who are unfaithful to you" (vv. 18-19).

Thus, "the way of the wicked will perish" (Ps. 1:6, ESV), because God knows and participates in the life of the wicked, though they go through life completely oblivious to his participation.

Pray: Dear Lord, my heavenly Father. I ask that you participate in my life at all times, so that, in that coming day of resurrection and judgement at the end of time, I may be found standing among the assembly of the righteous. I ask this in the Name of Jesus. *Amen.*

4

The Speech of Creation

> *1 The heavens declare the glory of God; the skies proclaim the work of his hands. 2 Day after day they pour speech; night after night they reveal knowledge. 3 They have no speech, they use no words; no sound is heard from them. 4a Yet their voice goes out into all the earth, their words to the ends of the world.*
>
> **Psalm 19:1-4a**

In Psalm 19, psalmist David sings about God's creation. He begins his song in v. 1 with a Hebrew literary device called a parallelism. This parallelism consists of *two lines* containing *three pairs* of similar terms:

(1) "The heavens	(2) declare	(3) the glory of God;
(1) The skies	(2) proclaim	(3) the work of his hands."

The *first pair* (1), "The heavens" / "The skies," are synonyms. Both point to what we see when we are out-of-doors and look up, with nothing hindering our view. In the daytime, we see the sun; in the nighttime, we see the moon and the stars.

The *second pair* (2), "declare" / "proclaim," are also synonyms. Both indicate speech or sound.

The *third pair* (3), "the glory of God" / "the work of his hands," however, are only partially synonymous. The first element, "the glory of God," is *defined* by or made explicit by the second element, "the work of his hands." If one could ask David what *is* "the glory of God" that he is talking about, David would explain, "It's *everything* that you and I can see when we look up into the heavens." In David's time, without the aid of any kind of telescope, on a very clear night he could have seen possibly up to about 10,000 stars (if he could have counted them). Now, in our time, the Hubble Telescope has detected at least 100 billion galaxies, and the more recent James Webb Telescope perhaps 200 billion!

Most peoples of David's time, with whom Israel interacted, traded and associated, worshiped *creation* rather than the God who created. Worshiping only what they saw with their physical eyes, they believed the sun, moon and stars to be gods. But, avows David, for the person who believes in the Creator God, there is a "seeing" revealed in the day and night that is beyond physical seeing. This "seeing" David calls "knowledge." One receives this knowledge through the "speech" of creation (v. 2).

David presents a paradox. He says of the created elements of the heavens, "They have *no speech*, they use *no words; no sound* is heard from them. Yet, *their voice* goes out into all the earth, *their words* to the ends of the world" (vv. 3-4), my emphasis). So, though creation does not speak, God has indeed put speech in creation. We do not normally refer to *seeing* speech, but of *hearing* speech. It is through hearing, then, that we *see* the God of creation. This is David's paradox.

In his earlier days as a shepherd in the fields and on the hillsides of Judea, David would have had many occasions for such spiritual perception. During those nights while watching his father's sheep, as he gazed upward at the star-lit heavens, with his heart open to hear God speak, he discovered something of the majesty of God "in all the earth" (Ps. 8:1, 9).

Yet, God, the Living Creator, knew that people, in the darkness of their hearts, would forget him. He knew that they would exchange "the truth about God for a lie," and would worship and serve "created things rather than the Creator" (Rom. 1:25). God knew that creation, alone, would be insufficient to direct people to himself.

So, God, the Living Creator, from time-to-time, chose to reveal himself personally to Israel's early leaders. To the Patriarchs Abraham, Isaac and Jacob he appeared as a living, personal God. Some generations later, Moses, the first of Israel's prophets, met face-to-face with God, coming to know him by his name *Yahweh*. And, through Moses the Lord gave Israel, prior to their entry into Canaan, his Written Law. This Law (which Israel came to know as the Law of Moses) contained all that God's people would need for a living relationship with God, the Living Creator.

Pray: Dear Lord, my heavenly Father. I ask today that I may hear you speak your Word to me through your Creation *and* through your Written Word. May I begin to see your majesty in all this earth in which I live. I ask this in the Name of Jesus. *Amen.*

5

The Benefits of God's Law

> *7 The law of the LORD is perfect, refreshing the soul. The statutes of the LORD are trustworthy, making wise the simple. 8 The precepts of the LORD are right, giving joy to the heart. The commands of the LORD are radiant, giving light to the eyes.*
>
> **Psalm 19:7-8**

Psalmist David speaks here of the rule of God's law over my life. I am to search the Creator God's Written Word for my life-code. This consists of the *principles* by which I am to live my life daily. If I do so, says David, I will experience great life-giving *benefits.*

Benefit One. "The law of the LORD is perfect, reviving a person" (v. 7a, my translation). The Hebrew word which the NIV translates as "soul" does not in this context refer to that part of my being that we usually think of as separate from one's body and which lives on after one's physical body has died. Rather, here it refers to my *whole being, a single unified entity* made up of my *body, soul and spirit,* that is, to *me*, "a person." To revive implies giving life to one who is near death. Thus, the Creator God's Written Word gives life to *my whole being.* Where once I was spiritually dead, now I am spiritually alive. This is basic. It is the foundation for the next benefit.

Benefit Two. "The statutes of the LORD are trustworthy, making wise the simple" (v. 7b). To receive this benefit, one must first be spiritually alive (Benefit One). Proverbs teaches that a right relationship with God is a prerequisite for receiving godly wisdom: "The fear of the LORD is the beginning of wisdom" (Prov. 9:10; see also 15:33). New Testament James instructs, "If any of you lacks wisdom, you should ask God, who gives generously to all" (Jas. 1:5).

Benefit Three. "The precepts of the LORD are right, giving joy to the heart" (Ps. 119:8a). Through obedience to God's Written Word, one finds reason to rejoice even in the midst of human tragedy. Elsewhere, psalmist David says, "Weeping may stay for the night, but rejoicing comes in the morning" (Ps. 30:5b). A psalmist of the Korah tradition found himself in great despair, yet affirms his hope in God, declaring, "at night his song is with me—a prayer to the God of my life" (Ps. 42:8b). New Testament Paul and fellow missionary traveler Silas found themselves locked in stocks in a Philippian jail. Yet, other prisoners overheard them in the middle of the night "singing hymns to God" (Acts 16:25). This attitude of one's heart leads to the next benefit.

Benefit Four. "The commands of the LORD are radiant, giving light to the eyes" (Ps. 119:8b), both spiritual and physical. When my heart rejoices, my eyes light up; when my heart is sad, my eyes become dull. On one occasion, Old Testament Saul's son, Jonathan, battle weary and hungry, found a hive of bees. With his staff, he dipped out a little honey, ate it, and "his eyes brightened" (1 Sam. 14:27). Just as honey was to Jonathan's physical eyes, so the commandments of God are to our spiritual eyes. With Apostle Paul, I pray that "the eyes of your heart may be enlightened" (Eph. 1:18).

Pray: Dear Lord, my heavenly Father. I ask that today I may experience the joy of knowing that I am stepping along in the light of your commands. Please give light to both my physical and spiritual eyes. I ask this in the name of Jesus. *Amen.*

6

The Law of the Lord

> *7 The law of the LORD is perfect, refreshing the soul. The statutes of the LORD are trustworthy, making wise the simple. 8 The precepts of the LORD are right, giving joy to the heart. The commands of the LORD are radiant, giving light to the eyes. 9 The fear of the LORD is pure, enduring forever. The decrees of the LORD are firm, and all of them are righteous.*
>
> **Psalm 19:7-9**

The Living, Personal, Creator God speaks to us in his Written Word. David calls this Written Word "the law of the LORD," which, he says, "is perfect, refreshing the soul" (v. 7). For psalmist David, "the law of the LORD" would have included at least the five books of Moses: Genesis through Deuteronomy.

After David's time, however, the Creator God added to his written law the other books of the Jewish Scriptures. All this we Christians call the Old Testament. Then God added the records of the beginnings of the Christian Church. These we call the New Testament. The Old and New Testaments combined comprises the whole Christian Bible. The whole of the Christian Bible is now the Creator God's Written Word.

If psalmist David were to live in our time, he would surely call this whole Bible "The law of the LORD."

The authors of the Old Testament books use several terms for God's Written Word. In Psalm 19, psalmist David uses six: "law" and "statutes" (v. 7), "precepts" and "commands" (v. 8), "fear" and "decrees" (v. 9).

These six terms, though close in meaning, are not exactly synonyms. Rather, *each is a part of the whole* of the Creator God's Written Word. The whole of the Written Word is like a precisely cut and highly polished diamond. Each facet, in its reflection of light, reveals only a *part* of the depth of the diamond's beauty. Only as one turns the diamond in the light, looking at each facet, does one begin to *see* and *know* the whole diamond. So, the diamond's total beauty is revealed only as one sees *all* the facets.

A diamond, however, is not a living thing. Though it is beautiful, it has no life-giving qualities. The Creator's many-faceted Written Word, however, contains life. It reveals to us the Living Creator God himself. When we read this Written Word, believe its teachings and accept them into our hearts, God speaks to our inner spiritual beings. With this inner, spiritual hearing comes spiritual knowledge of the Living Creator God.

The Old Testament speaks of knowing or acknowledging God (see Ps. 100:3; Hos. 6:6). The New Testament speaks of being born of God's Spirit (John 3:7-8). To know God, or to be born of God's Spirit, is to ask for and receive God's forgiveness for my sins and to allow God to be the Lord of my life. And, if God is the Lord of my life, I will seek to conform the conduct of my life to his "law," his "precepts" and his "commands."

Pray: Dear Lord, my heavenly Father. Without the help of your Holy Spirit, I find that I do not always seek to know what your will is for me. Help me to know and to live throughout today in your will. I ask this in the name of Jesus. *Amen.*

7

More Desirable than Gold

> *9 The fear of the LORD is pure, enduring forever. The decrees of the LORD are firm, and all of them are righteous. 10 They are more precious that gold, than much pure gold; they are sweeter than honey, than honey from the honey comb. 11 By them your servant is warned; in keeping them there is great reward.*
>
> **Psalm 19:9-11**

As my relationship with the Living Creator God deepens, so my love to know the precepts and commands found in his Written Word becomes a most desirable passion of my life. To know God's "decrees," says psalmist David, is "more precious than gold" and "sweeter than honey" (v. 10).

Gold was the most precious of metals known to David. Gold, however, cannot give life. Oh, yes, gold *seems* to give life for a moment. With gold I can buy possessions, power or position; I can buy influence in the high places of government. The seeking of gold may become the consuming passion of my life. But, when I pass from this earthly life, I take neither the gold nor its purchases with me. So, it is best that I live by the motto of our psalmist of Psalm 119, "The law from your mouth is more precious to me than thousands of pieces of silver and gold" (v. 72). Therefore, "I love your commands more than gold, more than pure gold" (v. 127).

Honey (Ps. 19:10), one of the few sweeteners known to David, was not easily obtained. Yet, it, too, cannot give life. Oh, yes, for a moment it *seems* to give life. When my body is exhausted and hungry, honey can strengthen me for the journey onward, but it cannot preserve my life forever. Again, it is best to affirm with our psalmist of Psalm 119, "How sweet are your words to my taste, sweeter than honey to my mouth" (v. 103).

But, says psalmist David, in keeping God's law, in making his Written Word the food of my spiritual life, "there is great reward" (Ps. 19:11). This reward is that I shall appear blameless, "innocent of . . . transgression" (v. 13), and, that the "words of my mouth" (my outward actions) and the "meditations of my heart" (my inward attitude)—together comprising my whole being—will "be acceptable in your presence, O LORD, my Rock and my Redeemer" (vv. 14, my translation).

Several hundred years after psalmist David's time, New Testament apostle Peter wrote: "So then, dear friends, . . . make every effort to be found spotless, blameless and at peace with [God]. . . . be on your guard so that you may not be carried away by the error of the lawless and fall from your secure position. But grow in the grace and knowledge of our Lord and Savior Jesus Christ" (2 Pet. 3:14, 18).

How do we maintain this steadfastness of life? How do we grow in the knowledge of Jesus Christ? By treasuring God's Written Word in our hearts!

Pray: Dear Lord, my heavenly Father. As I journey through today, may the meditations that I mull over in my heart be pleasing to you. And, please guide the words that come out of my mouth so that others may hear you speaking through me. I ask this in the Name of Jesus. *Amen.*

8

A Meditation on the Law of the Lord

> Psalm 119 is a 176-verse meditation upon God's Word. In this psalm an anonymous psalmist presents a standard by which we can know and walk in God's will. Our psalmist declares at the psalm's beginning, "Blessed are those whose ways are blameless, who walk according to the law of the LORD" (v. 1).
>
> **Psalm 119**

Psalm 119 teaches us that the Living God has spoken through, and revealed himself in, his written Word. And, since it is God who has revealed himself there, we believe this Word is true. Our psalmist affirms, "Your word, LORD, is eternal; it stands firm in the heavens" (v. 89).

This God who has spoken also must open our inner beings so that we can see and hear and understand his will. Thus, our psalmist prays, "Open my eyes that I may see wonderful things in your law" (v. 18). In a later time, Jesus, the Living Word, on the evening of the first day of his resurrection, accompanied two disciples on their walk from Jerusalem to Emmaus. As they walked along, writer Luke explains that Jesus "opened their minds so they could understand the Scriptures" (Luke 25:45). Some years later, Luke also writes of Philippian Lydia that "the Lord opened her heart to respond to [missionary] Paul's message" (Acts 16:14).

We learn in Psalm 119 that God must direct us in God's will that is revealed to each of us individually. Thus, our psalmist prays, "Direct me in the path of your commands, for there I find delight" (v. 35). But, as we walk in God's "path," we face much opposition from those who do not walk in God's ways. Our psalmist experienced the derision of "the arrogant" (v. 51), and thus affirms, "My comfort in my suffering is this: Your promise preserves my life" (v. 50).

Our psalmist experienced not only affliction as he lived according to God's word, but also great reward. He is "blessed" (v. 2), and is enabled to keep his way pure (v. 9). God's word keeps him from sinning against God (v. 11). "Good" comes out of affliction (v. 71); he has "hope" (vv. 74, 114-116, 147), and is not "put to shame" (v. 80). His "path" is lighted (v. 105), while his "eyes" cannot get enough of God's word (v. 123). Our psalmist's "ways are known to" God (v. 168) as his "tongue sing[s]" (v. 172). God's "hand" of "help" is present at all times (v. 173).

Pray: Dear Lord, my heavenly Father. Would you please reveal your will for me today, moment by moment, hour by hour. When I come to the end of this day, my I hear you whisper, "Sleep well, my faithful servant." I ask this in the Name of Jesus. *Amen.*

9

God's Word Blesses Us

> *1 Blessed are those whose ways are blameless, who walk according to*
> *the law of the LORD. 2 Blessed are those who keep his statutes and*
> *seek him with all their heart—3 they do no wrong but follow his*
> *ways. 4 You have laid down precepts that are to be fully obeyed. 5*
> *Oh, that my ways were steadfast in obeying your decrees! 6 Then*
> *would I not be put to shame when I consider all your commands. 7 I*
> *will praise you with an upright heart as I learn your righteous laws.*
> *8 I will obey your decrees; do not utterly forsake me.*
>
> Psalm 119:1-8

Our psalmist affirms that we who "walk according to the law of the LORD" receive God's blessing. As God observes our "ways" he deems them to be "blameless." God is not a faultfinder! (v. 1).

God's blessing comes when, with our combined external obedience and internal love, we seek both God's will and God himself "with a whole heart" (v. 2, my translation). Here, our psalmist echoes God's earlier command to the Israelites through his servant Moses, "Love the LORD your God with all your heart and with all your soul and with all your strength" (Deut. 6:5).

One of Israel's ancient songsters testified of God, "He is the Rock, his works are perfect, and all his ways are just. A faithful God who *does no wrong*, upright and just is he" (Ps. 32:4, my emphasis). Thus, our psalmist of Psalm 119 affirms that as we "keep [God's] statutes" and "follow his ways" God in turn keeps us from doing "wrong" (vv. 2-3).

Our psalmist says that the ways of this faithful and just God are revealed in his written word: "You have laid down precepts that are to be fully obeyed" (v. 4). He recognizes, however, that his own walk is not in full conformity with God's ways. So, he prays, "Oh, that my ways were steadfast in obeying your decrees!" (v. 5). He is asking that God would put within his heart the desire for full obedience.

"When I consider all your commands," says our psalmist, and walk in full obedience, your commandments free me from "shame" (v. 6). God's law is like a mirror, which, when I gaze into it, reveals to me my true self. Likewise, when I disobey, God's law shows me my sin and I am ashamed. This is intended to lead me to repentance. Then my shame is lifted.

God's word leads us to "praise" and worship. This becomes our natural response as God fulfills his word in us. Our psalmist declares, "I will praise you with an upright heart as I learn your righteous laws" (v. 7). In his worship, he includes a vow: "[O God,] I will obey your decrees; do not utterly forsake me" (v. 8). This, too, can be our vow. But we cannot keep such a vow in our own strength. We need God's helping grace.

Pray: Dear Lord, my heavenly Father. Assist me today to do or say nothing that will bring shame on your Name. At the end of this day, may I be able to look you in the face without shame. I ask this in the Name of Jesus. *Amen.*

10

God's Word Keeps Us on the Path of Purity

> *9 How can a young person stay on the path of purity? By living*
> *according to your word. 10 I seek you with all my heart; do not let*
> *me stray from you commands. 11 I have hidden your word in my*
> *heart that I might not sin against you. 12 Praise be to you,* LORD;
> *teach me your decrees. 13 With my lips I recount all the laws that*
> *come from your mouth. 14 I rejoice in following your statutes as one*
> *rejoices in great riches. 15 I meditate on your precepts and consider*
> *your ways. 16 I delight in your decrees; I will not neglect your word.*
>
> **Psalm 119:9-16**

The Bible places a high priority on moral purity of those of us who claim to be followers of the Lord.

We begin our journey of following the Lord with every intention of keeping our thoughts, intentions and actions pure. Occasionally, however, we find ourselves, as we journey along the path of life, acting in ways that are not pure or honoring to our Lord. Our psalmist is troubled by this, as he no doubt observes this, both in his own spiritual walk and in the walk of others. So he asks: "How *can* a young person stay on the path of purity?" (my emphasis). Surely his answer is

God-revealed: "By living according to your [God's] word" (v. 9).

It Is God's "word," then, that is our moral compass, that keeps us on the "path of purity." Our psalmist implies that the ideal time to begin to incorporate God's word into the fabric of life is while still in our youth. Then we may be spared years of continually falling off the path of purity. Our psalmist, of course, would recognize that some of us come to realize the values of God's word later or even late in life.

But to remain faithfully on that path of purity, our psalmist speaks of a partnership between him and God. From his side, it is a matter of the heart. He says, "I seek you [God] with all my heart." From God's side, it requires God's enabling grace. So he asks, "Do not let me stray from your commands" (v. 10). "When you see me straying from the path, God, nudge me back into its center!"

Our psalmist now reveals something of his personal habit in regard to the written word. God's word is not merely a once-a-week-listened-to word preached by his pastor. Nor is it merely something hidden in the unfamiliar pages of a Scroll or Bible sitting somewhere on a shelf in his home. No, affirms our psalmist, "I have hidden your word in my heart." This could happen only as he has read, and continues to read God's word again and again, until the very *words* of God's written word have become part of the fabric of his inner being. God's word then wells up from within, he testifies, in those times needed "that I might not sin against you" (v. 11).

God word is so much a part of our psalmist's everyday life that he cannot help but "recount all the laws that come from [God's] mouth" (v.13). This surely "implies a public declaring so that others may hear and know" (Thompson 2020, 302).

Our psalmist finds that following God's instructions as to how he should behave as he walks the path of life so fulfilling that he irrupts with this preposterous comparison: "In the way of your statutes I have rejoiced/rejoice as beyond all riches" (v. 14, my translation). John Goldingay quips, "fancy getting as much kick out of doing what Yhwh says as out of having all the wealth in the world" (Goldingay 2008, 388).

Pray: Dear Lord, my heavenly Father. Today, as I walk this path of life following you and your commandments, increase my love for your written word. As impure thoughts may arise, bring to my mind just the right "word" from your Word that will keep me from sinning against you. I ask this in the Name of Jesus. *Amen.*

11

God's Word Reveals Wonderful Things

> *17 Be good to your servant while I live, that I may obey your word. 18 Open my eyes that I may see wonderful things in your law. 19 I am a stranger on earth; do not hide your commands from me. 20 My soul is consumed with longing for your laws at all times. 21 You rebuke the arrogant, who are accursed, those who stray from your commands. 22 Remove from me their scorn and contempt, for I keep your statutes. 23 Though rulers sit and slander me, your servant will meditate on your decrees. 24 Your statutes are my delight; they are my counselors.*
>
> **Psalm 119:17-24**

Our psalmist prays to the Lord, "Open my eyes that I may see wonderful things in your law" (v. 18). "Law" for our psalmist was not merely a list of God rules, but the whole of the Scriptures available to him in his time. He might have in mind the five books of Moses—Genesis through Deuteronomy—and especially the mighty acts that God performed on behalf of his people recorded in those books.

The Hebrew word translated "wonderful things" elsewhere in the Psalms often refers to the miracles, signs and worders that God performed specifically against Egypt and the Pharaoh when delivering his people from their Egyptian slavery. These "wonderful things" would also include God's miraculous provision of food and water during the Israelites' forty years in the wilderness after escaping from Egypt up to their entry into Canaan.

Some people in our time view these "wonderful things" through human eyes only, seeing them merely as acts of nature. Others view them as mythological stories. We can rightly understand them as acts of God's power only as *he* opens our spiritual eyes. New Testament apostle Paul insists that spiritual matters can only be spiritually understood: "The person without the Spirit does not accept the things that come from the Spirit of God but considers them foolishness, and cannot understand them because they are discerned only through the Spirit" (1 Cor. 2:14).

God opens our eyes so that we can understand the world through which we are but travelers. Our psalmist says that he is only "a stranger on earth" (Ps. 119:19). Apostle Paul echoes this when he says of God's people that "our [true] citizenship is in heaven" (Phil. 3:20).

Having renounced the ways and values of the world, our psalmist requests of God, "do not hide your commands from me" (Ps. 119:19). God's ways replace the ways of the world. Only God's word can satisfy us.

Our psalmist has affirmed that his relationship with God is that of a "servant" who obeys his master's "word." As a servant, he has a right to expect God to reciprocate with care for his needs. Thus he asks: "Deal abundantly with your servant while I live, that I may keep your word" (v. 17, my translation).

As God's servant, our psalmist commits to "meditate on [God's] decrees," in which he takes "delight" (vv. 23-24). Because of this, however, "the arrogant" view him as fanatic and narrow minded (v. 21). They reject God's commandments, as did the mockers of Psalm 1. They heap "scorn and contempt" upon our psalmist and "slander" him (Ps. 119:22-23).

But, just as blessed persons of Psalm 1 do not find their directives for life from mockers, so our psalmist of Psalm 119 does not. Rather, it is as though God's "statutes"— God's directives—are personified, among whom he seeks counsel for the course of his life. These directives have become his "counselors" (v. 24).

Pray: Dear Lord, my heavenly Father. Today, I will live delightfully in subjection to your biblical directives. If others direct any slander or contempt against me because of this, help me to see such as minor in comparison to the contempt that your Son endured. I ask this in the Name of Jesus. *Amen.*

12

God's Word Enlivens Us

> *25 I am laid low in the dust; preserve my life according to your word. 26 I gave an account of my ways and you answered me; teach me your decrees. 27 Cause me to understand the way of your precepts, that I may meditate on your wonderful deeds. 28 My soul is weary with sorrow; strengthen me according to your word. 29 Keep me from deceitful ways; be gracious to me and teach me your law. 30 I have chosen the way of faithfulness; I have set my heart on your laws. 31 I hold fast to your statutes, LORD; do not let me be put to shame. 32 I run the path of your commands, for you have broadened my understanding.*
>
> **Psalm 119:25-32**

Here, our psalmist is despairing of life itself as he laments, "I am laid low in the dust" (v. 25a). What does he mean?

The Hebrew word translated "dust" here implies the "dirt" of the ground in which a dead body is buried or simply rots away to nothing (Goldingay 2008, 393). We see this in two other occurrences in the Psalms: (1) David laments, "you lay me in the dust of death" (22:15); (2) an anonymous psalmist says of God's animal creatures, "they die and return to the dust" (104:29). What has brought our psalmist of

Psalm 119 to this low point? He does not say. But he prays, "enliven me [lit. "make me alive"] according to your word" (v. 25b, my translation).

Is our psalmist speaking of near spiritual death, but in terms of physical death, and is asking for spiritual enlivening? Perhaps so. Spiritual enlivening is possible only when we have opened our hearts, confessing any wrongs revealed there. It seems that our psalmist has looked into his own heart and found "deceitful ways" (v. 29). Perhaps he has fallen into the trap of lying, and as one who is seeking to keep his way "blameless" (v. 1) and "pure" (v. 9), is asking God to remove such false ways from him.

God graciously responds, perhaps with words like, "Yes, my son, what would you have me do for you?" And our psalmist replies, "Teach me your decrees. . . . Cause me to understand the way of your precepts, . . . [to know that lying is incompatible with your way] . . . strengthen me according to your word [so that I tell the truth in all circumstances]" (vv. 26, 27, 28).

Our psalmist makes a deliberate choice: he rejects the way of deceitfulness (v. 29) and chooses "the way of faithfulness [or, "truth"]." And, to be reminded always of God's truth, he says, "I have set my heart on your laws" (v. 30). It is God's word that will restore our psalmist—and us—to truthful ways.

Having chosen the way of truth—perhaps in opposition to the "arrogant" who heap "scorn and contempt" upon him (see vv. 21-22)—our psalmist affirms, "I hold fast to your statutes, LORD," then pleads, "do not let me be put to shame" (v. 31). We hear our psalmist pleading, "O Lord, prove me right in the face of a world that insists that only foolish and weak people practice truth."

His faith strengthened, our psalmist increases the pace of his journey: "I run in the path of your commands, for you have broadened my understanding [lit. "my heart"]" (v. 32). Our "psalmist is no longer merely walking along; he is now a long-distance runner, in the race to complete the course!" (Thompson 2020, 306).

Pray: O Lord, my heavenly Father. As I continue to obey your word today, may I increasingly sense your trustworthiness. Continue to set my heart free to obey your word. I ask this in the Name of Jesus. *Amen.*

13

God's Word Teaches Us

> *33 Teach me, LORD, the way of your decrees, that I may follow it*
> *to the end. 34 Give me understanding, so that I may keep your law*
> *and obey it with all my heart. 35 Direct me in the path of your*
> *commands, for there I find delight. 36 Turn my heart toward your*
> *statutes and not toward selfish gain. 37 Turn my eyes away from*
> *worthless things; preserve my life according to your word. 38 Fulfill*
> *your promise to your servant, so that you may be feared. 39 Take*
> *away the disgrace I dread, for your laws are good. 40 How I long for*
> *your precepts! In your righteousness preserve my life.*
>
> **Psalm 119:33-40**

God has graciously enlivened our psalmist to spiritual life (Ps. 119:25). But our psalmist recognizes that he needs instruction. Thus he requests, "Teach me, LORD, the way of your decrees" (v. 33). We, too, following our forgiveness and spiritual renewal, need God to teach us so that we may continue on the road to spiritual maturity.

With teaching, however, must come understanding of what we are being taught. Thus our psalmist prays, "Give me understanding, so that I may keep your law and obey it with all my heart" (v. 34). As we seek understanding from God and obey what God shows us, our spiritual knowledge will increase throughout our lifetime.

In v. 35, our psalmist is now a soldier under orders, marching in step to the voice of his commanding officer who knows the way. So he prays, "Make me tread upon the pathway of your commands" (my translation). This is no side path that leads to nowhere, but a "pathway" that leads to a destination that the commanding officer knows well. And trusting fully in his commanding officer, our psalmist says of that "pathway," "Indeed, upon *it* I find delight!" (my translation, my emphasis).

Our psalmist realizes that he must know God's renewing, sustaining grace daily, that he cannot live today on yesterday's spiritual experience. Thus he prays, "Turn my heart toward your statutes" (v. 36a). He recognizes that the world is constantly trying to turn his heart (and ours) away. One such threat is the world's practice of "selfish gain" (v. 36b). This is gain or profit acquired at the expense of others, often the poor or the uninformed. Another of the world's threats is the desire for "worthless things" (v. 37a).

The Hebrew word translated "worthless things" here, is translated "an idol" (i.e., a false god) in Ps. 24:4, and "worthless idols" in one of God's heart-rending lamentations concerning "Virgin Israel": "My people have forgotten me; they burn incense to worthless idols, which made them stumble in their ways, in the ancient paths. They made them walk in byways, on roads not built up" (Jer. 18:13c, 16).

Most of us do not worship idols today. So, what might "worthless things" mean for us? It may mean the material must-have things that I see in the stores that I visit, appearing to have great value today. I buy them today, but throw them out tomorrow because "my eyes" have seen something bigger, prettier, or seemingly more useful. This is the ever-present threat of desire for "created things rather than the Creator" (Rom. 1:25).

Pray: O Lord, my heavenly Father. Today, turn my eyes away from even looking at the worthless things that clamor for my attention. Continually guide me in your way. I ask this in the Name of Jesus. *Amen.*

14

God's Word Gives Us Confidence

> *41 May your unfailing love come to me, LORD, your salvation, according to your promise; 42 then I can answer anyone who taunts me, for I trust in your word. 43 Never take your word of truth from my mouth, for I have put my hope in your laws. 44 I will always obey your law, for ever and ever. 45 I will walk about in freedom, for I have sought out your precepts. 46 I will speak of your statutes before kings and will not be put to shame, 47 for I delight in your commands because I love them. 48 I reach out for your commands which I love, that I may meditate on your decrees.*
>
> **Psalm 119:41-48**

It is God's "unfailing love" and "promise" (v. 41) that gives our psalmist confidence that he is on the right path in life as he continues stepping along, following God's commands, as we observed him so faithfully doing in our previous study (v. 35).

But, not everyone along the way applauds our psalmist's lifestyle. He speaks here of "my taunter" (v. 42, my translation). Earlier in Psalm 119, he has mentioned "the arrogant" who treat him with "scorn," "contempt" and "slander" (vv. 21-23). These are persons in his community who have chosen to reject God's law, who view our psalmist as narrow-minded. Even earlier in this psalm, our psalmist had affirmed to God, "I have hidden your word in my heart" (v. 11). He now calls this word "your word of truth." When a taunter steps out from a side path to attempt to deflect him from his path of righteous living, he can "trust" that this "word of truth" will rise up from his heart into his "mouth," that he might give his taunter a timely "answer" for why he has put his "hope in [God's] laws" (v. 42-43). If our Old Testament psalmist, through some kind of time warp, were to sit under New Testament apostle Peter's teaching, surely his heart would resonate with Peter's words: "Even if you should suffer for what is right, . . . Do not fear their threats; do not be frightened. . . . Always be prepared . . . to give the reason for the hope that you have" (1 Per. 3:14-15).

Thus, God's word, which our psalmist now calls "precepts," gives him "freedom" to "walk about" (v. 45) no matter the circumstances. This is the freedom of the follower of God who knows who he is and where he is going. Again, if our psalmist could have fast-forwarded in time and traveled about with New Testament apostle Paul, his heart would have resonated with Paul's words, "It is for freedom that Christ has set us free" (Gal. 5:1).

God's word that gives our psalmist freedom to come and go regardless of circumstances, also gives him boldness in witness. With God's "word of truth" in his mouth (v. 43), he "will not be put to shame," even when speaking of God's "statutes before kings" (v. 46). This freedom, however, is not absolute. Centuries later, Jesus anticipated a time when the freedom of his followers would be violated by those very rulers. He counseled his disciples, "On my account you will be brought before governors and kings as witnesses to them . . . But when they arrest you, do not worry about what to say or how to say it. At that time you will be given what to say, for it will not be you speaking, but the Spirit of your Father speaking through you" (Matt. 10:18-20).

Having been set free to follow his Lord, however God should lead, our psalmist speaks of four practices that govern his life. First, "I keep your law continually, forever and ever" (Ps. 119:44, ESV). This is no trial run. He is committed to this way of life right up to the time of death itself. Second, "I have sought out your precepts" (v. 45). Seeking speaks of a desire to know not only the precept itself, but why God requires it. Third, "I delight in your commands" (v. 47). Delighting speaks of joy and security. We delight in what we love. Thus our psalmist says "I love" God's "commands" (vv. 47-48). Fourth, "I lift up my hands for your commands" (v. 48, my translation). Here, our psalmist pictures his arms extended with the palms facing upward, indicating his readiness to receive. This is his physical affirmation of his devotion to God's word.

Pray: O Lord, my heavenly Father. As I travel along today's pathway, I extend my hands, palms turned upwards, ready to receive whatever you have for me. Whether it is blessing, trial or a chance to witness, assist me with your word to be faithful. I ask this in the Name of Jesus. *Amen.*

15

Our Psalmist Sings Songs in the Night

49 Remember your word to your servant, for you have given me hope. 50 My comfort in my suffering is this: Your promise preserves my life. 51 The arrogant mock me unmercifully, but I do not turn from your law. 52 I remember, LORD, your ancient laws, and I find comfort in them. 53 Indignation grips me because of the wicked, who have forsaken your law. 54 Your decrees are the theme of my song wherever I lodge. 55 In the night, LORD, I remember your name, that I may keep your law. 56 This has been my practice: I obey your precepts.

Psalm 119:49-56

Our psalmist depicts himself here in the role of a "servant" (v. 49) traveling about, perhaps doing business from place to place for his master, the Lord. Each night he takes lodging (v. 54) in the inns in the towns along his route that offer a night's bed, and breakfast before traveling on in the morning.

During the daytimes, however, as our psalmist travels along doing his master's business, he encounters those whose hearts are bent on doing evil against good people. He calls them "arrogant," persons of whom he says, "mock me unmercifully" (v. 51). Why? Their derision is directed at our psalmist's unwavering adherence to God's "law." Yet, even in the face of their mockery, he affirms, "I do not turn [aside] from your law" (v. 51).

These arrogant persons, are "the wicked, who have forsaken your law," our psalmist says (v. 53). They are those persons who, in another psalm, arrogantly scoff, "How would God know? Does the Most High know anything?" (Ps. 73:11). They are the same as the "fool," who, in still another psalm, "says in his heart, 'There is no God' " (Ps. 14:1). "Moreover, God's law—if God even exists!—has nothing to do with me. I will do as I please!"

These arrogant persons live in the short-view mode, as psalmist Asaph so well observes. He answers their arrogant challenge thrown into God's face with: "Surely you [God] place them on slippery ground; you cast them down to ruin. How suddenly are they destroyed, completely swept away by terrors!" (Ps. 73:18-19).

Our psalmist of Psalm 119, however, lives in the long-view mode. His view is based on a diligent knowledge of God's past intertwined dealings with the Israelites. He declares, "I remember, LORD, your *ancient laws*, and I find comfort in them" (v. 52, my emphasis). These "ancient laws" would include the whole history of God's acts of kindness to his forefathers recorded in the writings of Moses (Genesis–Deuteronomy). The remembrance of these "ancient laws," which our psalmist calls "your word to your servant," gives him "hope" (v. 49) throughout his travels.

But, whatever indignities we see our psalmist experiencing in the daytime as he travels about, in this portion of Psalm 119 (vv. 49-56) we hear our psalmist, perhaps with lyre or harp in hand, singing "songs . . . in the night" (vv. 54-55, ESV). In the darkness of the night, rather than dwelling on the evils of the daytime, our psalmist turns God's "decrees" into songs, that other lodgers may hear of the "name" of the Lord.

Pray: O Lord, my heavenly Father. I do not know what today holds for me as I journey through this day—joys or sorrows. But if sleeplessness should come in the night tonight, give me a song about your kindness and joys that I may sing. I ask this in the Name of Jesus. *Amen.*

16

God's Word Reveals His Love

> *57 You are my portion, LORD; I have promised to obey your words.*
> *58 I have sought your face with all my heart; be gracious to me*
> *according to your promise. 59 I have considered my ways and turned*
> *my steps to your statutes. 60 I will hasten and not delay to obey your*
> *commands. 61 Though the wicked bind me with ropes, I will not*
> *forget your law. 62 At midnight I rise to give you thanks for your*
> *righteous laws. 63 I am a friend to all who fear you, to all who follow*
> *your precepts. 64 The earth is filled with your love, LORD; teach*
> *me your decrees.*
>
> **Psalm 119:57-64**

Our psalmist's relationship with the Lord is built on mutual promise. Thus he says, "I have *promised* to obey your words. . . .[in return] be gracious [lit. "show favor"] to me according to your *promise*" (vv. 57-58, my emphasis).

This relationship of reciprocal obedience and grace began in an earlier time, when, our psalmist recalls, "I sought your face with all my heart" (v. 58). In our previous study (No. 15), our psalmist identified himself in the role of a servant. Perhaps he had somehow slipped up in his obedience to the "commands" (v. 60) of the Lord, his master. He does not say in what way or ways he had slipped up, but becoming aware of his shortcomings, he pleads, "I have sought your face with all my heart" (v. 58). There's nothing half-hearted in his confession of wrong-doing.

In our psalmist's ancient culture, for his master to have turned his face away would have signaled rejection, the withdrawal of his favor. Elsewhere in the Psalms, we hear an anonymous psalmist cry, "Hear my prayer, LORD; let my cry for help come to you. Do not hide your face from me when I am in distress. . . . My heart is blighted and withered like grass; I forget to eat my food" (Ps. 102:1-2, 4). Another psalmist laments, "How long, LORD? Will you forget me forever? How long will you hide your face from me? . . . Look on me and answer, LORD my God" (13:1, 3).

So, our psalmist of Psalm 119 reminds the Lord, "I have considered my ways"—ways which apparently were not in complete obedience to his master's "commands." Convicted by his master's grace (v. 58), he declares, "[I] have turned my steps to your statutes. I will hasten and not delay to obey your commands" (vv. 59-60). "My steps" is literally "my feet." "My feet" (v. 58), mentioned in the same context with "your commands" (v. 60), takes us back visually to v. 35. There we see our psalmist marching in step to the voice of his commanding officer who knows the way to their destination. As he marches in step, he prays, "Make me tread upon the pathway of your commands" (my translation).

God's commands are to be *walked* in. Our psalmist's haste (v. 60) reflects the intention of his *whole* heart (v. 58). When he has corrected his "ways," obedience has become his all-consuming passion.

The circumstance that prompts our psalmist's present cry for God's grace, he reveals, is that "the ropes of the wicked have ensnared me" (v. 61, my translation). These "wicked" are the same "arrogant/wicked" persons, whom he previously said unmercifully mocked him (v. 51) and who have turned their backs on God's law (v. 53). To ensnare with ropes refers to hunters who capture wild animals or birds with a rope snare. So, these "wicked" ones have metaphorically set a trap along the path our unsuspecting psalmist is traveling—and they have caught him! (v. 61a).

But the strategy of the wicked has failed. Our psalmist declares to God, "Yet, your law I have not forgotten" (v. 62, my translation). His relationship of reciprocal "promise" with God (vv. 57-58) holds him steadfast. "At midnight," perhaps with lyre or harp in hand and a song on his lips in the wayside inn where he has found lodging (see vv. 54-55), our psalmist rises from his bed. Why? He says, "To give you thanks" (v. 62). Thanks for what? That "The LORD'S covenant-love fills the earth" (v. 64, my translation).

Pray: O Lord, my heavenly Father. Today help me to live fully aware that I am your servant. Open the ears of my heart to hear clearly your wishes for all my thoughts, words and actions. Protect me from any person who would try to knock me off the path of following you. I ask this in the Name of Jesus. *Amen.*

17

God's Word Teaches Good Discernment

> *65 Do good to your servant according to your word, LORD. 66*
> *Teach me knowledge and good judgment, for I trust your commands.*
> *67 Before I was afflicted I went astray, but now I obey your word.*
> *68 You are good, and what you do is good; teach me your decrees. 69*
> *Though the arrogant have smeared me with lies, I keep your precepts*
> *with all my heart. 70 Their hearts are callous and unfeeling, but I*
> *delight in your law. 71 It was good for me to be afflicted so that I*
> *might learn your decrees. 72 The law from your mouth is more*
> *precious to me than thousands of pieces of silver and gold.*
>
> **Psalm 119:65-72**

Our psalmist reveals that he has experienced a temporary spiritual lapse as he's been traveling along life's path.

As God's servant (v. 65), he's been trying to obey his master will "with a whole heart" (v. 69, my translation). He confesses, however, to temporarily having gone "astray" (v. 67). The Hebrew verb translated "astray" points to making an error or sinning unintentionally. This unintentional straying, our psalmist says, happened "Before I was humiliated" (v. 67, my translation [NIV "afflicted"]).

The occasion of his humiliation, he reveals, were "lies" with which "the arrogant" (whom we met earlier in vv. 21-23, and 51) had "smeared" him (v. 69). They were telling lies *about* our psalmist! The lies, however, did not *cause* him to stray from the path. In fact, they had just the opposite effect. They *woke* him up to the reality that he had taken his eyes off the road (on which his Commander was leading him) and he was drifting towards a spiritual crash. Thus he testifies, "It was good for me to be humiliated" (v. 71, my translation). The occasion alerted him to his need to be always alert, concentrating on God's "decrees" (= instructions) for his daily life's journey (v. 71).

Our psalmist speaks of "good" six times in vv. 65-72: "Good you have done with your servant, O LORD" (v. 65, my translation); "Good discernment and knowledge teach me" (v. 66, my translation); "Good you are, and a doer of good" (v. 68, my translation); "Good it was for me that I was humiliated" (v. 71, my translation); "Good (NIV "precious") to me is the law of your mouth, more than thousands of gold and silver" (v. 72, my translation).

Our psalmist has learned in this present situation, that even though there is much evil heaped upon him by "the arrogant" ones (v. 69) lurking along his pathway of life, there is an even greater measure of good available to him from God who is with him *on* the pathway. He is learning to discern this good that God can bring out of the evil intentions of wicked persons.

Long before our psalmist composed this song of Psalm 119, his forefather patriarch Joseph learned such discernment. Concerning the evil his own blood brothers had perpetrated against him in his youth, when they sold him into Egyptian slavery (see Gen. 37), Joseph said to them years later, "As for you, you meant evil against me, but God meant it for good, to bring it about that many people should be kept alive, as they are today" (Gen. 50:20, ESV).

How do you and I acquire such spiritual discernment? By asking God, as our psalmist did: "Good discernment and knowledge teach me" (Ps. 119:66, my translation). The Hebrew word translated "discernment" here points to the meaning to "taste" or to "sense." The heart of our psalmist of Psalm 119 would resonate with psalmist David, who said, "Oh, taste (same Hebrew word as "discern") and see that the LORD is good!" (Ps. 34:8).

Pray: O Lord, my heavenly Father. As I travel along life's pathway today, I may encounter people who will speak evil things, hoping to persuade me to dwell on the hurt they intend to throw my way. Help me, teach me, rather to see that the good you intend for me is greater than any of their evil intentions. I ask this in the Name of Jesus. *Amen.*

18

God's Word Gives Us Hope

> *73 Your hands made me and formed me; give me understanding to learn your commands. 74 May those who fear you rejoice when they see me, for I have put my hope in your word. 75 I know,* LORD, *that your laws are righteous, and that in faithfulness you have afflicted me. 76 May your unfailing love be my comfort, according to your promise to your servant. 77 Let your compassion come to me that I might live, for your law is my delight. 78 May the arrogant be put to shame for wronging me without cause; but I will meditate on your precepts. 79 May those who fear you turn to me, those who understand your statutes. 80 May I wholeheartedly follow your decrees, that I may not be put to shame.*
>
> **Psalm 119:73–80**

Our psalmist does not visualize himself apart from his physical body; that is, his physical body is who he is. Moreover, he recognizes that he/his physical body did not simply materialize at the wave of a magic wand.

Thus, our psalmist affirms his awareness that it is *God* who is responsible for his existence when he says, "*Your hands* have made and fashioned me" (v. 73, ESV, my emphasis). John Hartley comments, "The word *fashion* suggests the arrangement of the parts of the body into an intricate structure" (emphasis original) (Hartley 1988, 415). Moreover, the word "made" points to God's creative activity when he "formed the man of dust from the ground and breathed into his nostrils the breath of life (Gen. 2:7, ESV). Our psalmist's words also echo Job's depiction of God at work fashioning Job as yet but a fetus in his mother's womb: "*Your hands* shaped me and made me. . . . you molded me like clay. . . . Did you not . . . clothe me with skin and flesh and knit me together with bones and sinews?" (Job 10:8-11, my emphasis).

Because of being one whom God has created, our psalmist is committed to traveling along life's pathway as God's loyal "servant" (Ps. 119:76). And, because of the two-way relationship between master and servant, he can fully expect God's protection. This protection is evidenced in God's acts of "unfailing love" and "compassion" (vv. 76-77).

Our psalmist asks for God's protection because he is still encountering "the arrogant," men who, just a few verses ago, were telling falsehoods about him (v. 69). Having failed with this approach, they now "subvert me with a lie" (v. 78, NASB 95), he says. Here, they are trying to beguile him about the truth of God's word.

In this, these arrogant men are true spiritual offspring of the serpent who beguiled Eve in Eden, when he said to her, "Indeed, has God said thus and so? Surely you cannot believe that God means what he says, do you?" (Gen. 3:1-5, my paraphrase). Unlike Eve, however, our psalmist is forewarned of the wiles of the serpent's offspring, and refuses to be beguiled. Rather, with his face turned toward his Creator, he affirms from past experience, "your laws are righteous" (v. 75), "your law is my delight" (v. 77). He then declares, "I will [continue to] meditate on your precepts" (v. 78), and follows with what may be taken as either a request or a statement of commitment: "May my heart always be without blame in regard to your statutes" (v. 80, my translation).

Earlier, our psalmist has asked of God, "May those who fear you rejoice when they see me, for I have put my *hope* in your word" (v. 74, my emphasis). Our psalmist's hope will encourage others to hope—other believers whose faith in God's word also is being subverted by mockers of God's promises.

New Testament apostle Paul requested of the believers at Thessalonica, "Pray that we may be delivered from wicked and evil people." He then affirmed to them, "the Lord is faithful, and he will strengthen and protect you from the evil one" (2 Thess. 3:1-3).

Pray: O Lord, my heavenly Father. Today, if I encounter someone who tries to convince me that I cannot trust your promises as given in your written word, give me wisdom and resolve to stand firm in your teachings. I ask this in the Name of Jesus. *Amen.*

19

God's Word Gives Us Hope—Again!

> *81 My soul faints with longing for your salvation, but I have put my*
> *hope in your word. 82 My eyes fail, looking for your promise; I say,*
> *"When will you comfort me?" 83 Though I am like a wineskin in*
> *the smoke, I do not forget your decrees. 84 How long must your*
> *servant wait? When will you punish my persecutors? 85 The arrogant*
> *dig pits to trap me, contrary to your law. 86 All your commands are*
> *trustworthy; help me, for I am being persecuted without cause. 87*
> *They almost wiped me from the earth, but I have not forsaken your*
> *precepts. 88 In your unfailing love preserve my life, that I may obey*
> *the statutes of your mouth.*
>
> **Psalm 119:81-88**

Our psalmist has fallen into the depths of despair while waiting in "hope" (v. 81) for God to rescue him from an apparent desperate situation as he travels life's pathway. Who has caused him such deep despair?

He speaks of "the arrogant" (v. 85). These are more of the same persons who have been relentlessly harassing our psalmist all along his life's journey (see vv. 21-22, 51, 69, 78). He describes them as those who live "contrary to [God's] law," and who, like hunters, dig "pits" "to trap" the unaware

(v. 85). It seems that our psalmist has temporally become trapped in one of their verbal pits. They seem to have twisted God's commandments in ways that have so trapped our psalmist in confusion that he can only cry out to God, "[I do believe that] all your commandments are trustworthy. With falsehoods they are persecuting me. *Help me!*" (v. 86, my translation, my emphasis).

Earlier, our psalmist has cried out to God, "My soul faints with longing for your salvation," (v. 81), and, "My eyes fail, looking for your promise" (v. 82). Both "faints" and "fail" translate the same Hebrew verb, which points to complete exhaustion. "Soul" represents our psalmist's inner being, "eyes" represent his physical body. His entire being, he is saying, is nearing collapse.

He reinforces his near collapse with the graphic cry, "I am like a wineskin in the smoke" (v. 83). Though the meaning of this metaphor is now lost in time, our psalmist may be likening himself to a skin bottle (used to hold either wine or water) that, for a long time, has been hanging in the smokiness of an Israelite house courtyard. It is now shriveled and cracked. In this nearly hopeless condition our psalmist cries out, "How long must your servant wait? When will you punish my persecutors?" (v. 84). "They [i.e., the arrogant] almost wiped me from the earth" (v. 87).

Yet, even in the depths of his despair, our psalmist never lets go of his confidence in God's word. "I do not forget your decrees," he affirms (v. 83). Moreover, "I have not forsaken your precepts" (v. 87). His appeal to God's "unfailing love" expresses his confidence that, in fact, God has not abandoned him to his enemies. God *will* preserve his life and lift him out of this pit into which he has become trapped, so that, he says, "I may *continue* to obey the statutes of your mouth [i.e., your spoken word!]" (v. 88, my translation, my emphasis).

Pray: O Lord, my heavenly Father. Today, with your help I determine to walk in the truth and trustworthiness of your promises. If I am tempted to solve any issue of right or wrong action in my own strength, remind me to ask for your help to make the right decision. I ask this in the Name of Jesus. *Amen.*

20

God's Word Enlivens—Again

> *89 Your word, LORD, is eternal; it stands firm in the heavens. 90*
> *Your faithfulness continues through all generations; you established*
> *the earth, and it endures. 91 Your laws endure to this day, for all*
> *things serve you. 92 If your law had not been my delight, I would*
> *have perished in my affliction. 93 I will never forget your precepts, for*
> *by them you have preserved my life. 94 Save me, for I am yours; I*
> *have sought out your precepts. 95 The wicked are waiting to destroy*
> *me, but I will ponder your statutes. 96 To all perfection I see a limit,*
> *but your commands are boundless.*
>
> **Psalm 119:89-96**

In our reading today, our psalmist recalls an experience in which, if it had not been for the power of God's "law" he surely "would have perished" (v. 92). God's "law" here is God's "word" of v. 89, which he affirms to be "eternal." It is eternal because it is firmly established in "the heavens," that is, the heavenly council from which God rules his creation.

Then, in v. 93, our psalmist speaks of God's "precepts," another term for God's word. In that harrowing experience when he would have perished, he recalls that it was these precepts that "preserved my life." They were "my delight," he exclaims. His implication is that he persisted in obeying God's ways—not deviating from them—and thus avoiding the pitfalls that would have caused him to spiritually fall.

But what was it that had so threatened our psalmist that he had despaired of life itself?

Our psalmist says, "*the wicked ones* have been lying in wait hoping to destroy me" (v. 95, my translation, my emphasis). We have met these brigands before in this psalm. They are those "arrogant" persons of vv. 21, 51, 69, 75 and 85, who have been harassing him from the start of his journey along the path of life. However, "Your word, LORD" (V. 89), that is, your purpose, your intention, which was determined in the heavenly council and spoken into existence, cannot be hindered or changed by the designs of these wicked men. Long, long ago, when time began, "you established the earth, and it [still] endures (v. 90). Our psalmist is looking back to God's initial act of creation—"the heaven and the earth" (Gen. 1:1). And, from "the beginning" until now, even though in that long ago time the wickedness of humanity had become so great on the earth, that God decided to destroy humanity from the earth with a great flood (see Gen. 6:5-7), "the earth" still "stands fast" (Ps. 119:90, ESV).

This observable "faithfulness" of God in the continuance of the earth is the same faithfulness that "continues through all generations" (v. 90) to those who "delight" in God's law (v. 92). These are those who "never forget [God's] precepts" (v. 93), who, in fact, seek out those very "precepts" (v. 94), and who "ponder [God's] statutes" (v. 95).

Yet, the earth, in fact, is *not* permanent. Jesus Christ, the One who spoke the universe into existence (John 1:3), affirmed that "Heaven and earth will pass away, but my words will never pass away" (Matt. 24:35).

Pray: O Lord, my heavenly Father. Today, as I journey along life's pathway, whatever opposition I may encounter from others who do not follow your ways, help me remember that it is *your* word, *your* precepts that will guide my steps with truthfulness and justice in all my dealings with others. I ask this in the Name of Jesus. *Amen.*

21

God's Word Gives Us Wisdom

> *97 Oh, how I love your law! I meditate on it all day long. 98 Your*
> *commands are always with me and make me wiser than my enemies.*
> *99 I have more insight than all my teachers, for I meditate on your*
> *statutes. 100 I have more understanding than the elders, for I obey*
> *your precepts. 101 I have kept my feet from every evil path so that I*
> *might obey your word. 102 I have not departed from your laws, for*
> *you yourself have taught me. 103 How sweet are your words to my*
> *taste, sweeter than honey to my mouth! 104 I gain understanding*
> *from your precepts; therefore I hate every wrong path.*
>
> **Psalm 119:97-104**

Our psalmist brackets Ps. 119: 97-104 with two strong opposing emotional terms: "love" and "hate." "Oh how I love your law!" (v. 97), he exclaims to God, "therefore I hate every false way" (v. 104, ESV).

In fact, our psalmist loves God's law so much that he declares, "I meditate on it all day long" (v. 97). "All day" may be a bit of an exaggeration, for surely he has other things that require his attention each day. Yet it reveals the *intent* of his heart as he carries out his activities throughout each day.

His continual meditation on God's "commands" does indeed give our psalmist wisdom beyond that of his "enemies" (v. 98). No matter what snare or trap they set to entice him away from the path God has set before him, he deflects them with God's word. These are real human enemies who have rejected God's regulations as having anything to do with the way they conduct their lives. Surely, however, if our psalmist could sit down with New Testament apostle Paul (which we really can picture them having done in the heavenly presence of Jesus!), he would agree with Paul that God's word in the heart and mouth of his servants also overcomes "the devils schemes" and "the spiritual forces of evil" (Eph. 6:11, 12).

I don't believe our psalmist is boasting when he says, "I have been given understanding, more than all my teachers, because your statutes are my meditation" (Ps. 119:99, my translation). He may well have sat under teachers who were teaching some of the latest philosophies of his day, but who did not anchor those philosophies in God's word. Unlike other students in his classroom, who, because of a lack of an intimate knowledge of God's word, were unable to discern truth from untruth, our psalmist was not deceived. Because of an in-depth knowledge of God's "statutes," he has been able to remained unswayed.

And, yes, God's word has even given our psalmist "understanding" far beyond the worldly wisdom of his "elders" (v. 100). From what he now says, these elders appear to be those who have learned the wisdom of "every evil path" (v. 101) and of "every false way" (v. 104, ESV). Such ways, he declares, "I hate" (v. 104).

In the wisdom gained from God's word, our psalmist follows a better way, learned from God himself; he declares,

"I have not departed from your laws, for you yourself have taught me" (v. 102). He compares the sweetness of the "words" with which God has taught him as more than the sweetness of the "taste" of "honey" in his "mouth." Perhaps our psalmist is referring to the effect that honey had on his physical body when exhausted and needing an energy boost! Just so was God's word to his lagging spiritual self when traveling along life's path.

Indeed, God is the master teacher. He teaches us through his word!

Pray: O Lord, my heavenly Father. Today, teach me as I read and meditate on your written word Impress upon my mind and heart the truths you know I need as I meet the challenges of others—my teachers, my co-workers—who make light of your requirements for living righteously. I ask this in the Name of Jesus. *Amen.*

22

God's Word Lights Our Path

> *105 Your word is a lamp for my feet, a light on my path. 106 I have taken an oath and confirmed it, that I will follow your righteous laws. 107 I have suffered much; preserve my life, LORD, according to your word. 108 Accept, LORD, the willing praise of my mouth, and teach me your laws. 109 Though I constantly take my life in my hands, I will not forget your law. 110 The wicked have set a snare for me, but I have not strayed from your precepts. 111 Your statutes are my heritage forever; they are the joy of my heart. 112 My heart is set on keeping your decrees to the very end.*
>
> **Psalm 119:105-112**

In vv. 105-112, our psalmist assures God that his entire "self" (v. 109, my translation; NIV "life") is in sync with God's requirements as he travels along life's pathway. He mentions his "foot" (v. 105, my translation; NIV "feet"), "mouth" (v. 108), "hands" (v. 109), and "heart "(v. 112) as, together, representative of his entire being.

God's "word" serves as "a lamp for my foot" (v. 105, my translation), our psalmist says. Though the NIV has "feet," our psalmist's Hebrew is singular. He has drawn this metaphor from physical life, and is fully aware that an olive oil lamp, carried in a lamp holder in his hand at his side, would cast light on his path for one step only—or one "foot"—at a time. Yet, this would be sufficient, for there would be light for the next "foot," and the next . . .

Just so, God's "word" gives spiritual light for one spiritual "foot" forward at a time as our psalmist walks the pathway of life. "The wicked" of v. 110 reappear from v. 61. They believe that our psalmist cannot clearly see the path ahead in the darkness. So, like hunters trapping an unsuspecting animal, they "set a snare" on his path. Watching for him to blithely step into their snare, they will snatch him from the path, his foot caught fast in its grip.

Ah, but God's "word," which our psalmist has "hidden in [his] heart" (v. 11), serves as a "lamp for [his] foot" (v. 105). It illuminates their snare just in time, allowing him to sidestep and keep going unscathed. Perhaps these wicked persons' attempt at entrapment is an enticement of ill-gotten riches such as the teacher/father of Proverbs 1 warns his student/son: "My son, if sinful men entice you, do not give in to them. If they say, 'Come along with us; let's lie in wait for innocent blood, let's ambush some harmless soul; . . . we will get all sorts of valuable things, and fill our houses with plunder; cast lots with us; we will all share the loot'" (Prov. 1:11-14). In the face of such enticements, our psalmist can testify to God with a clear conscience, "I have not strayed from your precepts" (Ps. 119:110).

It is the set of his will that enables our psalmist to resist such enticing temptations, as he further testifies to God, "I have set my heart to do your decrees to the very end" (v. 112, my translation). He settled this at an earlier time in life when he made his decision, "I have taken an oath and confirmed it, that I will follow your righteous laws" (v. 106). With his commitment, our psalmist claims his inheritance: "Your statutes are my heritage forever; they are the joy of my heart" (v. 111).

If we, too, set our hearts on keeping God's instructions, his word will illuminate the snares that the wicked may place in our path, both now and "to the very end" of our lives (v. 112).

Pray: O Lord, my heavenly Father. As I walk through this day, may your word give light for each step I take, each decision I make, and each word I speak. I ask this in the Name of Jesus. *Amen.*

23

God's Word Sustains Us

> *113 I hate double-minded people, but I love your law. 114 You are*
> *my refuge and my shield, I have put my hope in your word. 115*
> *Away from me, you evildoers, that I may keep the commands of my*
> *God! 116 Sustain me, my God, according to your promise, and I*
> *will live; do not let my hopes be dashed. 117 Uphold me, and I will*
> *be delivered, I will always have regard for your decree. 118 You reject*
> *all who stray from your decrees, for their delusions come to nothing.*
> *119 All the wicked of the earth you discard like dross; therefore I*
> *love your statutes. 120 My flesh trembles in fear of you; I stand in*
> *awe of your laws.*
>
> **Psalm 119:113-120**

Our psalmist speaks of both "hate" and "love" in the same breath (v. 113). It is "double-minded people" that he hates, and God's "law" that he loves (v. 113). Strong feelings, indeed!

These double-minded people our psalmist calls "evildoers" (v. 115). They are fellow Israelites whom one would expect to be loyal followers of Israel's God. But, alas! They are not! They are persons causing both moral and physical hurt to others among the community of believers. These evildoers have renounced all loyalty to what God requires. Our psalmist, however, keeps God's "commands" (v. 115).

Our psalmist has placed his "hope in [God's] word." As he faces new dangers from these evildoers, God is his "refuge [or, "hiding place"] and shield " (v. 114). His heart would surely resonate with psalmist David who affirmed of God, "In the shelter of your presence you hide them from all human intrigues; you keep them safe in your dwelling from accusing tongues" (Ps. 31:20). In still another psalm, David affirmed that when "The wicked draw the sword and bend the bow to bring down the poor and needy, to slay those whose ways are upright," God, acting as a shield, deflects their sword to "pierce their own hearts." God even causes the "bows" of the archers to "be broken," rendering their arrows ineffective (Ps. 37:14-15).

In Ps. 119, it is our psalmist's *love* for God's word that sustains him and upholds him in the face of all tests and attacks from the wicked. It is God's word that keeps *him* from falling into double-mindedness and straying from God's decrees. It is his faithful observance of God's commands that enables him to withstand evildoers to their face, sharply rebuking them: "Away from me, your evildoers" (v. 115).

It is still God's word today—treasured in our hearts—that enables *us* also to say to those who would seek to entice us away from God's commands, "Away from me, for in God are "my hopes" that will never "be dashed" (v. 116).

Our hope will never be dashed because, with New Testament apostle Paul, we affirm that "we have put our hope in the living God, who is the Savior of all people, and especially of those who believe" (1 Tim 4:10).

Pray: O Lord, my heavenly Father. Today, with the help of the Holy Spirit, may I not fall into double-mindedness. May I with single purpose and single heart follow your teachings in all my thoughts, in all my words, and in all my actions. I ask this in the name of Jesus. *Amen.*

24

God's Word—Loved More than Pure Gold

> *121 I have done what is righteous and just; do not leave me to my oppressors. 122 Ensure your servant's well-being; do not let the arrogant oppress me. 123 My eyes fail, looking for your salvation, looking for your righteous promise. 124 Deal with your servant according to your love and teach me your decrees. 125 I am your servant; give me discernment that I may understand your statutes.*
> *126 It is time for you to act, LORD; your law is being broken. 127*
> *Because I love your commands more than gold, more than pure gold,*
> *128 and because I consider all your precepts right, I hate every wrong path.*
>
> **Psalm 119:121-128**

Of the ten most expensive precious metals in our present-day world noted in a recently published listing (Ahmad 2023,np). none of them was known to our psalmist.

The Bible mentions six metals: gold, silver, lead, tin, copper, and iron. Of these, gold is mentioned more than 400 times. Silver comes in second at nearly 300 times (Voynick 2023, np). By this count, gold seems to have been considered the most precious. And so it seemed to our psalmist. In considering God's word, he assured God, "I love your commands [= God's word] more than gold, more than pure gold " (v. 127).

Simply "gold" is gold as it comes out of the ground, but "pure gold" is gold that has come through the high heat of the refiner's fire, its impurities removed. Our psalmist is saying, then, that God's word, tested in the crucible of the fires and heat of time, can be trusted to be true and accurate. God's word is more trustworthy than even the word of the most trusted of the gold refiners.

With refined gold one can buy position and status, possessions, houses and lands. The desire for these things can develop an intense desire for more gold. This intense desire can, in turn, lead to evil ways of acquiring gold by any means possible. Thus, we hear our psalmist complain to God, "Your law is being broken" (v. 126). Gold does not usually buy "what is righteous and just" (v. 121). Often it produces just the opposite: *un*righteousness and *in*justice!

With what, then, should one replace the desire for gold? One ancient Israelite teacher, lecturing to the young students in his classroom, says it is the desire for "wisdom," "knowledge and "understanding" that "the LORD gives." Listen in for a moment to his lecture: "If you accept my words and store up my commands within you, turning your ear to wisdom and applying your heart to understanding . . . and search for it as for hidden treasure, then you will understand the fear of the LORD and find the knowledge of God. For the LORD gives wisdom; from his mouth come knowledge and understanding. . . . Then you will understand what is right and just and fair—every good path" (Prov. 2:1-2, 4b, 5, 6, 9).

This ancient Israelite teacher also warned his students that "Those who trust in their riches will fall" (Prov. 11:28). Why? Because gold/money cannot guarantee security in life. It is here today but might be gone tomorrow, depending on the whims of the world's financial markets.

And so our psalmist has declared, "I love your commands more . . . than pure gold" (v. 127), and, "I consider all your precepts right" (v 128). It is his love for God's commands, his absolute trust in the rightness of God's precepts that enables him to "do what is righteous and just" (v. 121) when others all around him are breaking God's law (v. 126). It is God's invaluable "statutes" that "give [him] discernment (v. 125). It is God's "precepts" that puts within our psalmist a righteous "hate" for "every false way" (v. 128, ESV).

Pray: O Lord, my heavenly Father. Today, I ask the Holy Spirit to give me wisdom to see the falseness in any "get rich quick schemes" that may be put before me. Let my eyes not be blinded by the glitter of "gold" that does not store up for me treasure with you in heaven. I ask this in the Name of Jesus. *Amen.*

25

God's Words Give Light and Understanding to the Simple

> *129 Your statutes are wonderful; therefore I obey them. 130 The*
> *unfolding of your words gives light; it gives understanding to the*
> *simple. 131 I open my mouth and pant, longing for your commands.*
> *132 Turn to me and have mercy on me, as you always do to those*
> *who love your name. 133 Direct my footsteps according to your word;*
> *let no sin rule over me. 134 Redeem me from human oppression, that*
> *I may obey your precepts. 135 Make your face shine on your servant*
> *and teach me your decrees. 136 Streams of tears flow from my eyes,*
> *for your law is not obeyed.*
>
> **Psalm 119:129-136**

Our psalmist says God's "words" give "light" and "understanding to the simple" (v. 130).

"The simple," as most English versions say, may give modern readers the idea of a person of somewhat low or undeveloped intelligence. This is not what the Hebrew term implies, but rather "the inexperienced" (as in HCSB), or "the naïve."

Our psalmist, then, is speaking of the young who are not yet experienced in the ways of life "out there" in the streets and marketplaces of their towns. These inexperienced youth are those we encounter sitting under the instruction of the ancient Israelite teacher, who hopes his students will heed his warning of the moral dangers of the marketplace "out there." Listen in as he narrates this anecdote:

> While I was at the window of my house, looking through the curtain, I saw some naïve young men, and one in particular who lacked common sense. He was crossing the street near the house of an immoral woman, strolling down the path by her house. It was twilight, in the evening, as deep darkness fell. The woman approached him, seductively dressed and sly of heart. She was the brash, rebellious type, never content to stay at home. She is often in the streets and markets, soliciting at every corner. She threw her arms around him and kissed him, . . . "You're the one I was looking for! I came out to find you, and here you are! . . . Come, let's drink our fill of love until morning. . . ." He followed her at once, like an ox going to the slaughter. . . . So listen to me, my sons, and pay attention to my words. Don't let your hearts stray away toward her. Don't wander down her wayward path. For she has been the ruin of many; many men have been her victims. Her house is the road to the grave. Her bedroom is the den of death. (Prov. 7:6-27, NLT)

The naïve, then, are not equipped by experience to cope with what life will throw at them out there "on the streets." They are not yet able to discern wise responses from unwise.

But there is no need for the naïve to act foolishly, if they carefully heed God's teachings.

Our psalmist mentions that "The unfolding of [God's] words enlightens and gives discernment to the naïve" (v. 130, my translation). The plural "words" implies actual words written on a scroll. But those words are of no spiritual benefit to the naïve youth until "the unfolding"— or unrolling—of that scroll, so that God's words can be read, explained and absorbed.

Our psalmist also speaks of "those who love *your name*" (v. 132, my emphasis). These are those who have entered into an intimate relationship with God while still in their youth. This relationship gives them a basis for gaining wisdom in those situations where they as yet lack experiential knowledge. This life-changing relationship is the Old Testament equivalent of New Testament apostle John's words, "I write these things to you who believe in *the name* of the Son of God so that you may know that you have eternal life" (I John 5:13, my emphasis).

Pray: O Lord, my heavenly Father. Today, if Satan throws temptation at me as I travel life's path, give me wisdom to turn away from that temptation. Give me *your* strength to move straight forward, following *your* directions and commands. I ask this in the Name of Jesus. *Amen.*

26

God's Word Is Righteous

137 You are righteous, LORD, and your laws are right. 138 The
statutes you have laid down are righteous; they are fully trustworthy.
139 My zeal wears me out, for my enemies ignore your words. 140
Your promises have been thoroughly tested, and your servant loves
them. 141 Though I am lowly and despised, I do not forget your
precepts. 142 Your righteousness is everlasting and your law is true.
143 Trouble and distress have come upon me, but your commands
give me delight. 144 Your statutes are always righteous; give me
understanding that I may live.

Psalm 119:137-144

Our psalmist has bracketed this eight-verse stanza with an affirmation that God's "statutes . . . are righteous; . . . are always righteous" (vv. 138, 144). Moreover, he says, "they are fully trustworthy" (v. 138).

Our psalmist is convinced that God's own character guarantees the right-ness and trustworthiness of the statutes that he has issued, for we hear him say, "*You* are righteous, LORD" (v. 137, my emphasis), and, "*Your* righteousness is righteous eternally" (v. 142, my translation, my emphasis).

Out of his own righteousness, then, God has issued his "promises," which equal his word. These promises, our psalmist says, "have been thoroughly *tested*" (v. 140, my emphasis). The Hebrew word translated "tested" also means "refined," as in the process of smelting gold or silver in fire's heat, removing the dross and impurities. We find this word in another psalmist's metaphorical application of this process to God's dealing with the Israelites in the wilderness: "For you, God, tested us; you *refined* us like silver" (Ps. 66:10, my emphasis).

As God's "servant" (Ps. 119:140) traveling along life's pathway, our psalmist encounters "trouble and distress." Yet, he finds "delight" in God's "commands" (v. 143). To delight in God's commands is to delight in God himself. Our psalmist would find a kindred heart in psalmist David, who said, "Take delight in the LORD, and he will give you the desires of your heart. Commit your way to the LORD; trust in him and he will do this: He will make your righteous reward shine like the dawn" (Ps. 37:4-6).

Not only does our psalmist delight in God's word, he has tested God's promises and "loves them," for he has come to know that God's "law is true" (Ps. 119:140, 142, 143). Moreover, although "my enemies ignore your words," he says to God, " I do not forget your precepts" (vv. 139, 141).

Our psalmist is always seeking to learn. Thus, he pleads with God, "give me understanding that I may live" (v. 144). With an ever deepening understanding of God's statutes, promises, laws, precepts, words, and commands, he will be able to live more fully in step—one foot forward at a time—with God's plan for him.

Pray: O Lord, my heavenly Father. As I set out on my journey with you today, as I put one foot forward at a time, clarify my understanding of what *your* plan is for me. Enable me to live fully under your guidance with each breath I take. I ask this in the Name of Jesus. *Amen.*

27

God's Word Is Eternal

> *145 I call with all my heart; answer me, LORD, and I will obey*
> *your decrees. 146 I call out to you; save me and I will keep your*
> *statutes. 147 I rise before dawn and cry for help; I have put my hope*
> *in your word. 148 My eyes stay open through the watches of the night,*
> *that I may meditate on your promises. 149 Hear my voice in*
> *accordance with your love, according to your laws. 150 Those who*
> *devise wicked schemes are near, but they are far from you law. 151*
> *Yet you are near, LORD, and all your commands are true. 152*
> *Long ago I learned from your statutes that you established them to*
> *last forever.*
>
> **Psalm 119: 145-152**

There is nothing half-way or timid in our psalmist's call for the Lord's help. Physically he is all in with his "[whole] heart" (v. 145), his "eyes" (v. 148) and his "voice" (v. 149). For some time, it seems, he has been pleading with the Lord, "answer me" (v. 145), "save me" (v. 146), and—desperately—"preserve my life, LORD" (v. 149).

Why is our psalmist so desperate? Because he is being threatened by persons whose purpose in life is to "devise wicked schemes" (v. 150). Prophet Isaiah speaks of persons who "make up evil schemes." He calls them "scoundrels"!

They are those who "destroy the poor with lies, even when the plea of the needy is just" (Isa. 32:7). This points to corrupt courts of the land, before whose judges the needy cannot get a fair hearing.

These schemers, our psalmist says, "are far from (God's) law"; they have complete disregard for God's law (Ps. 119:150). They consider God's law not applicable to how they live their lives! We've met these fellows earlier in our studies: as "mockers" (Ps. 1:1) for whom God's law is meaningless, and as "the arrogant" who, "with malice" and "arrogance" scoff at God, saying, "How would God know? Does the Most High know anything?" (Ps. 73:3, 8, 11).

So desperate is our psalmist that he rises even before the morning light has come to cry out for God's help. Indeed, he has been awake "through the watches of the night" (lit., "my eyes have met the night watches") waiting in "hope" for God to fulfill his "word." But his waiting has not been idle waiting, for he uses this time of wakefulness to meditate on the Lord's "promises" (Ps. 119:147-148).

As our psalmist meditates on the Lord's promises during those wakeful hours of the night, he is reminded of the Lord's "love" (v. 149; "steadfast love" [ESV, NRSV]; "faithful love" [CSB]; "loyal love" [my translation]. The Hebrew word behind *this* word for love defines the very essence of who the Lord *is*. Because he *is* loyal love, our psalmist is assured that the Lord will "hear my voice" (v. 149). Moreover, because of *the Lord's* near presence (v. 151), though surely under great pressure from the nearness of those who spurn and disobey the Lord's law (v. 150), he is not overwhelmed.

What holds our psalmist steady in such adverse circumstances? He's been on this journey of life for a long time. He's no novice at spiritual danger. Thus, he affirms to the Lord, "All your commands are true. Long ago I learned from your statutes that you established them to last forever" (vv. 151-152). Your word was true and dependable when I began this journey. It is so even now and will still be true and dependable when I pass from this earthly life to my eternal home.

You and I, too, may be assured of God's nearness and the eternal dependability of his word.

Pray: Oh, Lord, my heavenly Father. As I continue on my journey in life today, I am assured that your promises and your Presence surround me. Whatever I may encounter along the way, your Presence is greater than anything or any person that may oppose my following your commands. I ask this in the Name of Jesus. *Amen.*

28

God's Word Is Truth

> *153 Look on my affliction and deliver me, for I have not forgotten*
> *your law. 154 Defend my cause and redeem me; preserve my life*
> *according to your promise. 155 Salvation is far from the wicked, for*
> *they do not seek out your decrees. 156 Your compassion, LORD, is*
> *great; preserve my life according to your laws. 157 Many are the foes*
> *who persecute me, but I have not turned from your statutes. 158 I*
> *look at the faithless with loathing, for they do not obey your word.*
> *159 See how I love your precepts; preserve my life, LORD, in*
> *accordance with your love. 160 All your words are true; all your*
> *righteous laws are eternal.*
>
> **Psalm 119:153-160**

Our psalmist is suffering persecution at the hands of "wicked" men, his "foes" he calls them (vv. 153, 155, 157). These men are "faithless" because they live a lifestyle that utterly disregards God's "word" (v. 158). Another unnamed psalmist aptly described such men: "He boasts about the cravings of his heart; he blesses the greedy and reviles the LORD. In his pride the wicked does not seek him; in all his thoughts there is no room for God" (Ps. 10:3-4).

Three times our psalmist pleads with God, "preserve my life"—"according to your promise" (119:154); "according to your laws" (v. 156); "in accordance with your love" (v. 159; "your steadfast love" [ESV]; "your loyal love" [my translation]). This plea indicates that our psalmist fears that his very life is in danger from these faithless foes who are persecuting him. After all, these men have rejected God's "decrees" (v. 155) and God's "word" (v. 158), as having anything to do with the way they carry out their daily lives. When they see a person living in step with *God's* rules, anger rises from their hearts to action against such piety. Goodness like *that* must be destroyed!

Not only is the persecution of our psalmist physical, but we can detect sustained attempts to sow doubt in his heart about the trustworthiness of God's "word"—"You don't *really* believe that what God has said can be trusted do you? You don't believe that God *really* exists, do you?"

But our psalmist is convinced that God's requirements of his servants are not arbitrary dos and don'ts issued at the whims of a fickle God, whose moods change with the weather. Rather, they originate in God's very nature which is "love" (v. 159; see Study 27). They are *love*-rules, issued with the very best in God's heart for our psalmist.

So, our psalmist does not give in to his persecutors. His unshakeable conviction concerning God's *word* is that, "All your words are true; all your righteous laws are eternal" (v. 160). No matter what his persecutors say, as our psalmist has traveled life's highway, time and again, God has proven the truth of word. He will not throw away his confidence!

Pray: Oh Lord, my heavenly Father. As I set out on today's journey in life, I do not know what or whom I may encounter. I may meet someone who has rejected anything having to do with you and living a Godly life. In the moment of those possible encounters, I ask that the Holy Spirit assist me to respond with wisdom and kindness. At the same time, give me courage to stand firm in the truth of your Word. I ask this in the Name of Jesus. *Amen.*

29

God's Word Gives Great Peace

> *161 Rulers persecute me without cause, but my heart trembles at your*
> *word. 162 I rejoice in your promise like one who finds great spoil.*
> *163 I hate and detest falsehood but I love your law. 164 Seven times*
> *a day I praise you for your righteous laws. 165 Great peace have*
> *those who love your law, and nothing can make them stumble. 166*
> *I wait for your salvation, LORD, and I follow your commands. 167*
> *I obey your statutes, for I love them greatly. 168 I obey your precepts*
> *and your statutes, for all my ways are known to you.*
>
> **Psalm 119:161-168**

Our psalmist is again experiencing persecution from "rulers." We first encountered these persecuting rulers early on in vv. 22-23, where they were treating him with "scorn," "contempt" and "slander." Here, they are persistently attempting to convince him of the "falsehood" of God's "law." They detest him for his high regard for God's "word." Moreover, they simply can't stand someone who *rejoices* in God's promises (vv. 161-163).

It seems that our psalmist often publicly expresses his love for God's law and his statutes, and that he obeys God's precepts and statutes. He speaks of praising God "seven times a day" for his "righteous laws" (vv. 163-168). His persecutors are bent on stamping out such piety!

"Great peace" is a benefit of loving and keeping God's law (v. 165). "Peace" is *shalom*, a completeness or wholeness. It is a wholeness of relationship between God and me, and between my neighbor and me. Prophet Isaiah tells us that "those whose minds are steadfast, because they trust in" the Lord, are rewarded with "perfect peace (lit., *shalom shalom*)" (Isa. 26:3). When we listen in on the Proverbs teacher, we hear him advising his students, "My son, do not forget my teaching, but keep my commandments in your heart, for they will prolong your life many years and bring you peace/*shalom* and prosperity" (Prov. 3:1-2).

This relationship between God's law as the guide of one's life and a resulting peace is not a teaching newly conceived by our psalmist and the Proverbs teacher. It is squarely rooted in the Mosaic Law. When God declared to Israel through Moses the blessings of obedience, he had promised, " 'If you follow my decrees and are careful to obey my commands, . . . I will grant peace/*shalom* in the land, and you will lie down and no one will make you afraid.' " Moreover, God guarantees this peace by his own presence: " 'I will walk among you and be your God, and you will be my people' " (Lev. 26:3, 6, 12).

Note again that our psalmist says that he praises God "seven times a day" (Ps. 119:164). The number seven indicates completeness throughout the Old Testament. So, in spite of the persecutions of those who rule, he praises God while he works, while he walks the streets of his town, while he eats, while he plays—in *all* circumstances. New Testament apostle Paul put it this way, "Rejoice in the Lord always. . . .

And the peace of God, which transcends all understanding, will guard your hearts and your minds in Christ Jesus" (Phil. 4:4, 7).

Pray: Oh Lord, my heavenly Father. I have no idea what circumstances I may encounter today as I set out on life's journey. Whatever they may be, I ask that the Holy Spirit may hold my mind and heart steadfast on you, with a peace that only *you* can give. I ask this in the Name of Jesus. *Amen.*

30

God's Word Gives a Song

*169 May my cry come before you, LORD; give me understanding
according to your word. 170 May my supplication come before you;
deliver me according to your promise. 171 May my lips overflow with
praise, for you teach me your decrees. 172 May my tongue sing of
your word, for all your commandments are righteous. 173 May your
hand be ready to help me, for I have chosen your precepts. 174 I long
for your salvation, LORD, and your law gives me delight. 175 Let
me live that I may praise you, and may your laws sustain me. 176 I
have strayed like a lost sheep. Seek your servant, for I have not
forgotten your commands.*

Psalm 119:169-176

We come now to our psalmist's final six verses of this longest Old Testament psalm. In these verses he reveals his deepest longing and affirmation of full and complete trust of his Lord: "May my lips overflow with praise" (v. 171) and "May my tongue sing of your word" (v. 172).

Our psalmist has revealed to us in the previous verses of this psalm the many troubles that he has experienced as he has been traveling along the pathway of life's journey, as a servant following the commands of his Lord, his Master.

These troubles have included enemies at all levels of his society, betrayal of members of his community, snares, traps and arrows that he compares to those of hunters and fowlers, sicknesses, dishonesty and lies, and much more.

Yet the cry of his heart is that, in spite of all these adverse circumstances, on his "lips" and "tongue" always may be heard a song of "praise" for God's "word." God's word is promise and command, and it gives our psalmist "delight" (vv. 170-174). For this he praises! For this he sings!

Throughout the Old Testament Psalms there are at least forty-three occurrences where the psalm writers link singing and praising, as though synonymous activities. Thus, praises are to be sung.

The singing of praise, in turn, is often linked with giving praise, as in: "I will praise you, LORD, among the nations; I will sing of you among the peoples" (57:9).

Such songs are to be sung with joy, as in: "Then my head will be exalted above the enemies who surround me; at his sacred tent I will sacrifice with shouts of joy; I will sing and make music to the LORD" (27.6).

Some psalmists urge that we sing such songs to the accompaniment of musical instruments, as in: "Praise the LORD with the harp; make music to him on the ten-stringed lyre. Sing to him a new song; play skillfully, and shout for joy" (33:2-3).

We are to sing in praise of God's "righteousness" (7:17), "strength" (21:13), "love" (59:16), and "wonderful acts" (105:2). We are to: "Praise the LORD, for the LORD is good; sing praise to his name, for that is pleasant" (135:3).

Why does our psalmist of Psalm 119 sing praises? Because, he says, "all [God's] commands are righteous" (v. 172).

In the final verse of Psalm 119 (v. 176), our psalmist "identifies himself as still Yahweh's 'servant' . . ., who still adheres to his masters 'commands.' Yet somehow he senses a derailment in his life's spiritual walk, so pleads with Yahweh, "Just as you would seek 'a lost sheep,' don't abandon me. 'Seek your servant' " (Thompson 2020, 343).

Pray: Oh Lord, my heavenly Father. As I begin today's journey I praise you that you stand ready to come to my help at any moment. If I begin to stray like a lost sheep, nudge me back into the path you have set before me. Today I *delight* in all that you are asking me to both be and do. I pray this in the Name of Jesus. *Amen.*

Made in the USA
Columbia, SC
03 January 2024

29097228R00054